Zana goes Spear Fishing

This book was funded by
The Global Environment Facility Small Grants Programme and
implemented by the United Nations Development Programme
in collaboration with the Coastal Zone Management Unit Barbados.

Published by Trekvoy Art & Literary Services
www.facebook.com/The Zana Series
www.thezanaseries.com
Copyright 2015 The Zana Series
The Zana Series is a Trademark of Trekvoy Art & Literary Services
ISBN-13: 978-1517167974

T.A.L.E.N.T®
Trekvoy Art & Literary Endowment for the
Naturally Talented

"Good Morning Zana, would you like to go spear fishing with me?"
Mr. Hubble asked.
"Yes! I would like to go".
She said.
"It is a beautiful day to go to the beach".

Mr. Hubble makes sure that everything is packed.

Two wet suits.
Two masks.
Two spears.
Two buckets.
Two towels.

Mr. Hubble is going to teach Zana how to hunt for lionfish.

Lionfish do not belong on the coral reef in Barbados. They have been eating all the other fish. They also damage the coral reef.

At the beach, Zana and Mr. Hubble change into their wet suits. The suits will keep them safe and warm.

Mr. Hubble shows Zana how to use the spear. He tells her how to handle the lionfish. "They have long spines that can hurt you" says Mr. Hubble. "Be careful".

They put all the things they packed on to the boat.

Off they go!

"This is a good spot to look for lionfish"
says Mr. Hubble.
He puts the anchor down so that the boat will not float away.

Zana and Mr. Hubble dive
into the water.
They are good swimmers.

Mr. Hubble catches his first lionfish.
He shows Zana.

Zana remembers everything Mr. Hubble said about the lionfish.
She is very careful.
She does not touch them.
Zana catches one with her spear.

"Help! Help!"
Zana and Mr. Hubble look
around quickly.
They see a little fish
calling to them.

Zana and Mr. Hubble swim over to the little fish. "How can we help you?" Zana asked. "My sister is trapped in a big box and I cannot get her out".
The fish cried.

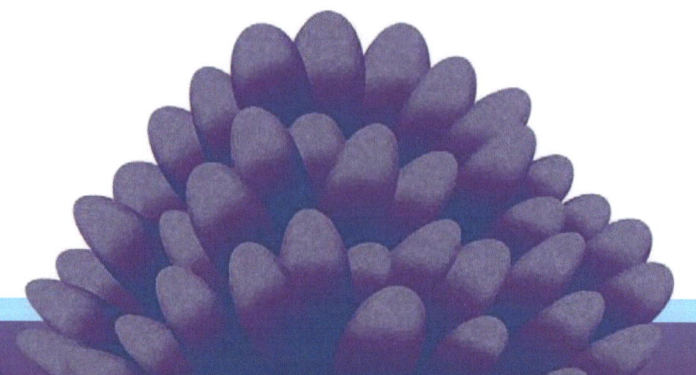

He shows them the big box. "It is a fish trap that someone forgot here". Mr. Hubble said. "It looks like it has been here for a very long time".

"A lionfish wanted to eat me" said the fish inside of the trap. "I swam in here so I could hide but now I cannot get out".

Mr. Hubble looks at the trap to see how he can free the little fish.

He uses the sharp edge of his spear to cut a hole in the trap. The little fish swims out.

The two little fish are happy again.
They thank Mr. Hubble and Zana for their help.

Mr. Hubble takes the trap back to the shore. That way no other sea animals will get trapped.
Zana and Mr. Hubble had a good day spear fishing.

Now it is time to eat.
They share their food with
other friends from the
swamp.
The catch of the day is
Grilled Lionfish
with Breadfruit.

Ghost Fishing

This happens when fish traps that are lost or forgotten at sea. They stay underwater trapping fish inside of them.

For more information on this topic visit me at:
thezanaseries.com

DO YOU KNOW?

The lionfish is known as an invasive species in the Caribbean. Invasive means to invade and take over a place that does not belong to you.

www.ingramcontent.com/pod-product-compliance
Lightning Source LLC
Chambersburg PA
CBHW041519280526

45792CB00004B/1311